Drama Workshop

Teaching Drama to Beginning Actors

❖ ❖ ❖

by
Chuck Neighbors

Drama Workshop

Teaching Drama to Beginning Actors

Copyright © 2019 Chuck Neighbors

Portions of the book were previously published
under the title *Drama Now!* by Chuck Neighbors
(Lillenas Publishing 2005)

All rights reserved. Except for the pages labled "Handouts," no portion of this book may be reproduced in any form without permission from the publisher, except as permitted by U.S. copyright law.

For permissions contact: chuckneighbors@gmail.com

All rights reserved.

ISBN:9781695208230

Cover photo by Mauricio Keller from Pixabay

CONTENTS

1	Why Am I Doing This?	1
2	Getting Started	3
3	Acting Basics - Inhibition	8
4	Acting Basics - Body Control	11
5	Acting Basics - Body Movement and the Stage	18
6	Acting Basics - Eye Focus	24
7	Acting Basics - Vocal Projection	29
8	Acting Basics - Diction	31
9	Acting Basics - Memorization	34
10	Acting Basics - Characterization	38
11	Putting it All Together	46
	Handouts	47
	Acknowledgements	54
	About The Author	55

Chapter 1

Why Am I Doing This?

Since 1975 I have made a career of performing and teaching drama. I've conducted my drama workshops for hundreds of theater groups, schools, churches and conferences on five continents around the world. All good stuff!

But there is a problem. While a few of the places that hosted the workshops have qualified directors and individuals with theatre experience, many do not; and those who do have training are usually only a fraction of those that will actually be doing the performing.

One of the questions that I am asked most frequently is, "How do we get started?" My answer is always, "You need to hold a drama workshop."

Ideally, you would hire a professional to come in and conduct the workshop for you. Indeed, that has been one of the things I have enjoyed doing. It is a great idea to have a guest instructor conduct the workshop—even if you already have a qualified director/teacher in your midst. Why? In a word: reinforcement. Almost without fail, every time I conduct a workshop the local drama director affirms that one of the best things to come out of the workshop is the fact that having me teach has given credibility to the things they have been teaching. They say, "Now they will believe me when I tell them they have to turn toward the audience or project their voice more, etc." This, and the fact that the team is being trained at all, is a great reason to have someone from the outside conduct the workshop.

But what if you can't afford someone else or don't know who to get in your area? That is the reason for this resource. I believe that if you have a little bit of experience as a performer or actor, and perhaps have taken a drama class or two, you can conduct this workshop yourself. And please note, while this book is written primarily for directors, it can also serve as a good hands-on resource for the actor, serving to reinforce and remind individual performers of the basics of acting. I have also used this workshop as both an audition and/or first rehearsal for many productions that I have directed.

You'll find that this workshop practically teaches itself. Your role is more that of a facilitator than that of a teacher (although there are a few places that you will have to play the role of teacher). The workshop is participatory with a "learn-by-doing" approach. It is exercise-driven and most of the "teaching" is done in the discussions following the exercises. I have strived to make the exercises as simple to follow as possible. Each exercise will contain:

Purpose—makes it clear why you are doing this activity.

Do This—instructions to you, the facilitator, in setting up the exercise.

Say This—gives you a sample of how to give instructions for the exercise.

> ***Side Coach***—*if applicable, for instructions and tips to give out while the exercise is being done.*
>
> ***Variation***—*if applicable, an alternate way to try the exercise.*

DEBRIEF — A time to stop, gather with your actors and talk about what you've just done; share insights and applications; and how they could improve on the skills highlighted in the exercise.

The workshop accomplishes several things:

- It will serve as basic training for your actors. Even if you have team members with previous experience in theatre, the workshop will get everybody on the same page in terms of structure, vocabulary and procedures.
- The workshop gives you an opportunity to establish the rules of the stage and rehearsal and define the roles of the actor and the director.
- This is also a great time to scope the talent in your group. It will serve as informal audition.
- Finally, the experience is a great team-building exercise. The very experience of being together for a day of intense activity will accomplish much in unifying your team and building trust among the members.

The whole event is meant to be fun, interactive and a time of discovery for you and your team.

Chapter 2

Getting Started

This workshop is designed as a day-long event and should be able to fit nicely in to a six-hour block with a break in the middle for lunch. Alternately, you could offer it as a course over several sessions; however, if you do, I would strongly suggest that they be successive days rather than one day a week. You'll find that the team members will retain the training better if it is more intensive. One of the major benefits of the workshop model is the community that is built over the time spent together. That is much easier to achieve in the one-day model.

Since we want to build community among team members, be sure to allow time for informal visiting. This happens well over food and beverage. Setting up a continental breakfast is a great way to set the tone. Be sure to provide nametags if there will be people present who do not know the rest of the participants.

> The day could look something like this:
>
> | | |
> |---|---|
> | 8:45 AM | Continental breakfast |
> | 9:00 | Session begins |
> | Noon | Break for lunch |
> | 1:00 PM | Session resumes |
> | 4:00 | Session ends |

Introduction

Give the group a brief overview of the day, but avoid talking too long here. Set the tone for the day by DOING something. A good mixer is a great way to start. Keep in mind that every exercise will have a purpose. Here is a good mixer to start off the session:

Mingle Mosey

Purpose: To mix up the group, allowing them to meet others. Begin breaking down inhibitions. Getting to know others.

Do This: Divide the room into two equal groups.

Say This: You on the right side of the room are now the "Mingle Family." Your name is now your real first name combined with your new last name, Mingle. The same instruction for the other half of the room, the "Mosey Family." Now the Mingles are going to meet the Moseys. I want you to mill around the room and introduce yourselves to as many people as possible. After awhile I will yell, "stop" (or "freeze"); at that time the person you are greeting will become your partner. If for some reason you do not have a partner, raise your hand and look for someone else with their hand raised and partner with that person. (If the number does not come out evenly you can form a group of three or you could put yourself in the exercise to make it work.)

Tip: This is a good time to explain a rule that you will use through out the day. Since there will be lots of interactive activity going on all day, you'll want to establish a method of getting everybody quiet without screaming at them--to save your voice. This is a method you may have learned in kindergarten but it is still effective with adults. Instruct the group that if you need them to quiet down you will simply raise your hand. If they see your hand raised they are to close their mouths and raise their hands. If everyone follows instructions you'll find the room gets quiet fairly quickly. Rehearse this once with the group.

Do This: Give them some time to "mingle mosey" and then stop and have them partner up. Once everyone has a partner, you give them an assignment. Remember these assignments will have an application to drama, but we will get to that later.

First Assignment: Fret and Fuss

Say This: I want you to think of something that irritates you: a pet peeve or something that makes you upset or angry. Now, I want you to share that with your partner for one minute (time them). Begin.

(You will notice most people will simple be telling their partner about the thing that upsets them. This is not the goal. You want them to feel that emotion—this is acting, after all! Stop them and renew the instruction)

Stop! Hold it! I think you misunderstood. I want you to really get into it. Red faces, angry gestures, wild emotion! And remember and that people who are upset are not very good listeners. Don't listen to your partner—both of you fret and fuss at the same time. Now, try it again.

Do This: After the minute is up, stop the group and perhaps give a little commentary about communication: "We are not very good listeners when we are upset. Today is not only about drama but also understanding that good drama also mirrors real life aspects of communication."

Set them in motion with Mingle Mosey again and after a few moments stop and have them partner up again.

Second Assignment: Top Three List

Say This: Now I want each person to think of three things that they are most thankful for. You again have one minute to share those things with your partner (you don't really have to keep time on this one). This time I really do want you to listen to what your partner has to say.

Do This: Let them share the information. After they have gone for a minute stop them. Take a moment to point out the difference in the sound of the room as compared to the Fret & Fuss exercise. Also note the difference in how they were communicating with each other in contrast to Fret & Fuss.

Hopefully, you will notice a difference in the group at this time. The ice is broken and people are a bit more relaxed and comfortable. Have everyone take their seats and move on to the next step.

DISCUSSION:

Why Are You Here?
Why Drama?
What Does It Take To Make It Work?

Why Are You Here?

Now we move into a discussion time where we will establish our focus for the day. Depending on the size of the group we might go around the room and have everyone introduce themselves and perhaps give a sentence or two about why they came to the workshop (love drama, like entertaining people, a friend twisted my arm). If the group is not too large, you could also mix in something interesting to help us get to know each other like "tell us a hobby or something that nobody else in the room knows about you." This gives you, the leader, a better understanding of just who you are working with.

Why Drama?

This is a very important discussion where you will explore the purpose of drama in the life of our community/culture. Don't panic; you are likely to discover that the group will give you all the answers that you are looking for. But in short, the answers you are looking for and are likely to hear from the group are (in no particular order):

- Cultural relevance
- We remember and learn by seeing as well as hearing
- We live in an entertainment-oriented culture and are accustomed to getting our information through the arts
- We are a storied people and we learn through story
- People identify with characters they see on stage, which makes for powerful communication
- Provides a way for people to use their talents and gifts
- It's fun!

Feel free to expound on these observations. Having people own these reasons will help them understand and appreciate their talents and gifts.

What Does it Take to Make it Work?

Here is a chance at the outset to help people identify some of the things that are going to be required to have a successful drama group. The goal is to help people realize that good drama doesn't just happen. It takes work, planning, and discipline. So again, in discussion mode, ask people to list what they think it is going to take. Here are some of the answers you are looking for (again in no particular order):

- People
- Material (scripts)
- Rehearsal space
- Leadership/Director
- Commitment
- Costumes, sets, and props
- Technical support: lighting, sound, sets, props, etc.
- Good communication between the drama team leader and other leaders in your organization

At the end of the day or at your next meeting you may want to craft a vision statement for your drama group. The two discussions you have just had will set up the foundation for that statement.

Tip: *A Special Guest!* This is a great time in the workshop to have a word of greeting and encouragement from another leader in your organization (school principle, pastor, head of a fine arts department). If possible, it would be excellent if they would participate in the whole day—just to get an understanding of what goes into making drama work, if for no other reason. But to at least show up and give a word of encouragement and endorsement will help elevate this in the minds of those attending. It makes the statement that "this is important to the life organization." Giving voice to the vision and mission of the greater organization, and how drama is a part of that, will go a long way in validating your efforts!

Now let the fun begin!

Chapter 3

Acting Basics — Inhibition

One of the first obstacles to getting started for beginning actors is fear. Fear of getting up on stage and making a fool out of themselves, fear of blowing their lines, fear of not be accepted by their fellow actors or by the audience. We need to tackle this fear head on. One of the best ways to do that is through games designed to break down inhibition. Acting involves taking risks and before I can expect actors to take risks in front of an audience they need to be comfortable taking them in front of the rest of the team. These exercises are designed to do just that. And remember, you can use these exercises not only for this workshop but for future rehearsal times as well.

Loosening Up and Stretching Exercises

Purpose: To loosen up the group, and their bodies, both at the same time. To get the actors in the mindset that acting is a physical activity not just a verbal one.

Do This: Have everyone stand in a large circle. Have them spread out so there is plenty of room between people.

Say This: To get started we need to understand that acting is a physical activity. We are going to spend much of our time today using our bodies, so we need to get them limbered up and ready to perform.

Do This: Lead the group in several stretching exercises. Stretch upward on tiptoes like they are going to touch the ceiling. Then flop over like a rag doll, bending at the waist. Do this a couple of times. Now from the rag doll position have them stand up slowly as if they are a marionette being pulled upright by strings attached to various parts of the body.

Now start everyone shaking their right hand. Then add their left hand. Now expand to shaking the whole arms and keep adding: the feet, the body, the head. Now keep doing this and make a vocal sound at the same time.

Finally, do some isolation exercises. Have them drop their heads forward and then slowly roll the head around their shoulders, rolling to the left for a couple circles and then to the right. Next, do circles with the shoulders: first the right, then the left, then both at the same time. You could keep going: add the hips, bend and rotate from the waist, do the legs and the feet.

Copycat

Purpose: To break down inhibition, break the ice, get people comfortable doing things in front of each other.

Do This: Have everyone stand in a large circle. Have them spread out so there is plenty of room between people.

Say This: I know you are all probably afraid that I am going to somehow make you look like a fool today. The fear of looking like a fool is very common among performers. One of the best ways to get over that fear is to make everyone look like a fool at the same time so nobody feels self-conscious about it. To do that we are going to play a game called Copycat. The rules are quite simple. I am going to start by doing something crazy, like acting like an animal, making weird noises, silly movements—really anything that comes to mind. So that I don't feel foolish doing this I want you to do exactly what I am doing at the same time—just like a copycat! After I have seen that everyone is copying me I will point to someone else in the circle and they will do the first thing that pops in their head and we will all copy them. And we will just keep tossing it around the room for awhile. Because we are all going to be doing this, really the only people who should feel foolish are those who are not participating! Let's begin.

> ***Side Coach***: *Encourage people to just do the first thing that comes to mind. Be spontaneous. Don't waste time "trying to think of something"—just do it! Encourage people to use sound and movement together. The more outlandish, the better.*

Yes, Let's!

Purpose: To break down inhibition. To encourage spontaneity and imagination.

Do This: Have the actors spread out over the room. They need to find some space that is not too close to someone else.

Say This: Now we are going to use our imagination like when we were little children playing all by ourselves. For this game it might help you to think of yourself as back in kindergarten. I am going to call out an activity like this: "Let's ride a bike." I want you to all answer back in unison "Yes, let's!" Then I want you to go into your own little world and pretend you are riding a bike. Don't watch others, you don't have to interact with anyone else—it's just you riding a bike. Then after we have all done that for awhile, someone else in the room calls out a new activity and we all again respond in unison with, "Yes, let's!" and immediately pretend to do that activity. We will keep this going until we have done several different activities.

(Sample activities: brushing teeth, playing basketball, climbing a mountain, etc.)

> ***Side coach:*** *Don't watch everyone else—just do your own thing. Keep encouraging new activities after we have done one for 10 seconds or so. Use the whole room--you don't have to stay in one spot.*

DEBRIEF

After you have done this series of exercises it is time to talk about it. This is where the actors begin to see why we did what we did and then learn from the experience. So encourage everyone to take a seat and ask the following questions for discussion:

Q: What was the purpose of those exercises?

Q: What has happened to the atmosphere in the room since doing those exercises?

Q: When we first started, if I were to ask somebody to act like, say, a monkey, I probably would not have gotten many volunteers. But now if I asked somebody, do you think people would be more likely to comply? Why?

Chapter 4

Acting Basics — Body Control

It may surprise you and your team, but we are going to spend quite a bit of our day focused on body control. Proportionately, probably about half of the workshop time will deal with the physical aspects of acting. Why? Acting is a visual medium. Our bodies are instruments to be used to communicate our message. Often what we say with our bodies is just as important as the lines we recite. Actors need to become aware of this and learn to use and train their bodies to say what we want them to say. The next group of exercises will help us grasp this concept.

The first thing we need to do is to get people in small groups of 4 or 5. You can do this in a number of ways, counting off or forming groups close to where they are sitting, but that is so mundane! Let's instead continue to reinforce the inhibition theme and group people with a game called ….

Barnyard

Purpose: To divide people into groups in a way that helps breakdown inhibitions and also facilitates people working with others that they might not usually choose. Building community.

Do This: Figure out how many groups you will need in order to have 4 or 5 people in each group. Come up with the names of animals that correspond to that number of groups. For example if you want 5 groups then you could have: cow, horse, chicken, sheep and pig.

Say This: In order to put you into groups, I am going to come around, point at you and call you the name of an animal. Remember the animal but please don't take it personally (go around and assign the names). Now, making only the *sound* of your animal, find everybody that is the same animal as you.

Do This: Now that people are in groups, you need to spread the various groups out in the room so that they have some room to work independently of each other. You are now ready for the first group assignment.

Variation: *You could do this exercise with songs, foreign accents or famous people impersonations.*

(Note: There will be several group assignments during the day. If the place you are meeting has adjoining classrooms, you may want to use them as an option for group assignments when they are preparing things to be performed throughout the day)

Group Pantomimes

Purpose: To illustrate how we can communicate without words. To build teamwork in small groups.

Each group will be given an assignment to be performed as a group. Depending on the number of people and time constraints, you could have each group do every kind of pantomime, or to expedite things you can give each small group a different kind of pantomime. I usually end up doing the latter.

Do This: In advance prepare some lists. I'll get you started but you can easily customize this and create your own. The lists are:

- *Household machines*: sewing machine, toaster, washing machine, lawn mower, vacuum cleaner
- *Things that happen in nature*: sunset, waterfall, tornado, leaves falling, flowers blooming
- *Abstract machines*: love, fear, prejudice, confusion, apathy

Say This: I am going to come around to each group and give you an individual assignment. (Each group will have a different assignment, so do this secretly.) The idea is to work as a group to create a pantomime that communicates the thing assigned to your group. There is no talking or noises allowed in the performance of these pantomimes. You will need to work fast as you will only have about 3-5 minutes to prepare. After the time is up we will all come together and perform the pantomimes for each other.

Do This: Go around to each group and assign the various things. Perhaps two groups perform household machines, two do things from nature and two do abstract machines. The abstract machines take a little more explanation and are a bit more challenging. You might want to assign the abstract machines first in order to give those groups a bit more time. The abstract machines can be explained as machines designed to communicate the abstract ideas. They can be resemble a familiar machine (car, assembly line, washing machine) or unlike anything we have ever seen before. The main goal is to communicate the abstract only using our bodies. After you have assigned, allow them the time allotted to complete the task.

Side Coach: *Remember these performances are to be done silently in pantomime. You are to all be a part of the thing you are creating NOT the person using or affected by the creation.*

After the time is up you are ready for the first real performances of the day. Assemble the group back together as an audience and perform the pantomimes for each other. The audience is encouraged to guess what each thing is but make sure each group completes its pantomime rather than stopping because somebody guessed the right thing.

Tip: This first performance is a good place to teach a little audience etiquette—and church audiences need to be taught these things. Encourage applause at the end of the performance. Remind the different groups that this is not a time to continue fine-tuning their upcoming performance—no talking! They need to give the performers 100% of their attention.

DEBRIEF

Some questions to discuss:

Q: What have you learned from this experience?

Q: How was it working with your group?

Q: What was the most challenging part of the exercise?

The things you want to emphasize are the ways that they communicated ideas without words, using only their bodies. Also build in the idea of teamwork. They worked together to create these performances—they relied on one another to get the message across.

Michaelangelos

Purpose: To show how our bodies communicate messages. To encourage creative expression.

This is one of my favorite workshop exercises! I like it because it not only gives an opportunity to teach, but also because it is a concept that is easily adaptable into a performance piece. It is a tried and true technique that is used by many drama instructors. It also goes by the names of Potter and Clay, and Tableaus. The basic idea is to build sculptures or tableaus based on ideas that you give to the group.

Do This: Once again you will need a list, prepared in advance, of about five ideas to be turned into sculptures. Here are some suggestions, but feel free to create your own:

- Enthusiasm
- Prejudice
- "Do unto others as you would have them do unto you" (The Golden Rule)
- Scene from a familiar story like a fairy tail or a parable

Instruct everyone to get back into their small groups from the pantomime.

Say This: We are now going to do an exercise called Michaelangelo. One person from each group will become "Michaelangelo," a sculptor. The others in the group will become lumps of clay. Michaelangelo will make a sculpture of an idea that I am going to give you using the "lumps of clay" to make his/her art. This is a non-verbal exercise, so no talking is allowed by either Michaelangelo or the lumps of clay. You will only have one minute to make this sculpture so think and work fast. Go from the first impulse that hits you—chances are that if you thought about it for five minutes you would do pretty much the same thing anyway. Each person will get a chance to do one of these, and they get harder as we go along…so who is going to be the first volunteer in your group (each group selects who in their group will go first)? Okay, the first word I am going to give you is "enthusiasm." You have one minute. Go!

Tip: When explaining how the sculpture is done, use a volunteer as a lump of clay and demonstrate how you can sculpt them. Move their body into several poses. Show how you can create facial expressions, focus the eyes (by pointing where you want them focused), etc. This example will help people to get it very quickly. Also, be aware and sensitive to the fact that this exercise requires a lot of physical touch, which brings in another aspect of inhibition.

> *Side Coach:* Remember--no talking! Don't tell them what to do--mold them. Lumps of clay, you need to concentrate. Try not to laugh. You have 30 seconds. You have 15 seconds. You have 5 seconds. Freeze!

Do This: At the end of the minute tell everyone (except the Michaelangelos) to freeze. Then tell the Michaelangelos to imagine that they are in a museum and to walk around and see what other people have created to communicate enthusiasm. Pick what you consider the best sculpture. After the Michaelangelos have viewed all the sculptures, tell everyone to unfreeze (except the one you have selected) and to come over and look at the one you have selected. Now as a group you are going to analyze this one sculpture.

Say This: What is it about this sculpture that communicates the idea of enthusiasm?

As people discuss what they see, you will discover opportunities to share insight into how our bodies communicate. In order to sculpt "enthusiasm," we had to tap into what it looks and feels like. Raised arms, smiles, cheers, big eyes, mouths open. All these things that are part of communicating one simple word have tremendous application to the acting process.

After you have identified as many things as you can, tell the actors to unfreeze. You then move back to the groups to do the next sculpture, repeating the above instructions. Before each one begins use each new sculpture to teach and add elements of good stage pictures. Things to include are:

> ➢ Establish a point of view. Where do people stand to view this art? Compare this to work on stage.
> ➢ Make sure everyone can be seen. Don't let people block (stand in front of others so they can't be seen by the audience) each other in the sculpture. Don't have people stand with their backs to the audience.

- Straight lines are boring. Make your art three-dimensional. Avoid placing people in straight lines; instead build triangles with the bodies on stage.
- Levels are interesting. Have some people sit, some stand and some kneel for intriguing pictures.
- Include touch and eye contact with the individuals in the sculpture, if appropriate.
- When it comes to story, think contrast and conflict. Everybody standing with their arms in the air does say "enthusiasm." But we have *story* if we take one person out and make them sad. Now there is something happening that is interesting to watch rather than everybody doing the same thing.

Additional things to layer into each new sculpture:

- For the "prejudice" sculpture think about contrast. This is a good one to show different attitudes and build the idea of story.
- For the Golden Rule sculpture encourage eye contact and touch.
- For the story scene, remind people that there are many scenes in this story (most people want to do the last scene). Encourage variety.

DEBRIEF

Once again, we have used our bodies to get ideas across without spoken word. Ask these questions:

Q: What did you learn/observe from that exercise?

Q: Was it difficult to hold one position for a long period of time?

Q: As you created these scenes, where did the pictures you sculpted come from?

This is an exercise that can be easily turned into a performance! By simply memorizing a few positions in a tableau, you can create powerful images in front of an audience. Ask the group to brainstorm some ideas for using this. Some ideas I have used or heard of are:

- Sculptures based on a poem, a scripture or a short story (a different picture for different verses or ideas.)
- Sculptures to a song that has strong imagery. Think in terms of "moving pictures."
- Sculptures that illustrate a helping in the family or community. An example might be a sculpture showing people in cleaning up a park, people serving others, people visiting the sick, etc.
- A fun teaching tool in the classroom. Children love to do this exercise and would enjoy it as a visual aid in teaching almost any story.

The point is to be creative and use this as a springboard for performance. This is also a good "first performance" for actors, as it can get them in front of any audience without the stress of memorizing lines.

Chapter 5

Acting Basics—Body Movement and the Stage

No, I am not being redundant here. Body control and body movement are two different things.
Body Control has to do with becoming aware of our body and how it can be used to communicate. Body Movement has more to do with the rules of the stage (yes, there are rules!). This is where we will get into the proper way to stand, sit, and walk on stage. We will deal a bit with what to do with our hands, how to use props and some other things that will help us look good in front of an audience. While a character we portray on stage can express a lot with posture and movement, too often we will look just like ourselves on stage rather than the character. It is best to start from a neutral position and way of movement and then layer on the character rather than to fall into the trap of always moving the way we are used to in real life!

This section is going to be a brief overview that can fit nicely into our format of a one-day workshop; however these "rules" need to become habits and that takes more practice and time than we can accomplish in a one-day seminar. This is also the one section of the workshop that is more lecture-driven. If you feel uncomfortable with this area then you can choose to hit it very lightly for now, but do know that you will need to obtain the knowledge and pass it on to your group if you want to do your very best in performance.

The Stage

First let's begin with the stage (see diagram). There are nine basic areas of the stage (some theatres use more but for most productions nine will be sufficient). These areas serve as your compass to navigate the stage. Stage directions are always given from the perspective of the actor standing on stage, facing the audience. Stage right is to the actor's right, stage left is to the actor's left. Down stage is the area closest to the audience. Upstage is the area farthest away from the audience. Some areas are stronger than others. Obviously the closer to the audience and the more centered you are on the stage will establish a stronger connection with the audience. So, from strongest to weakest, the areas are: Down Center, Center, Down Right, Down Left, Right, Left, Up Center, Up Right, Up Left. (There is a another picture of this diagram in the back of the book. You may want to duplicate it and use it as a handout to the participants.)

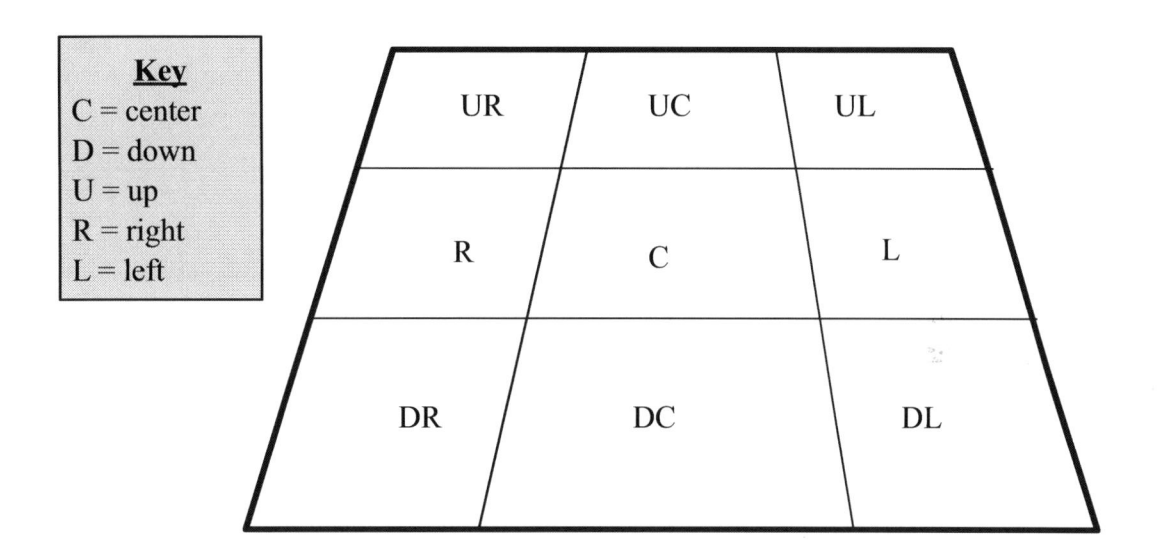

Key
C = center
D = down
U = up
R = right
L = left

UR	UC	UL
R	C	L
DR	DC	DL

AUDIENCE

Do This: After explaining the stage areas ask for a volunteer to come to the front of the room. Establish an area that will be your stage and then call out random stage areas and see if the volunteer can move to the correct location. Try it with several volunteers to make sure the actors understand.

Stance

Now that we understand the stage and stage directions, we need to talk about proper stance on stage. It is very important for actors to understand this simple rule: Always stand on stage with your upstage foot forward. That is to say your foot that is farthest away from the audience should be slightly ahead of the one that is closest to the audience (see diagram).

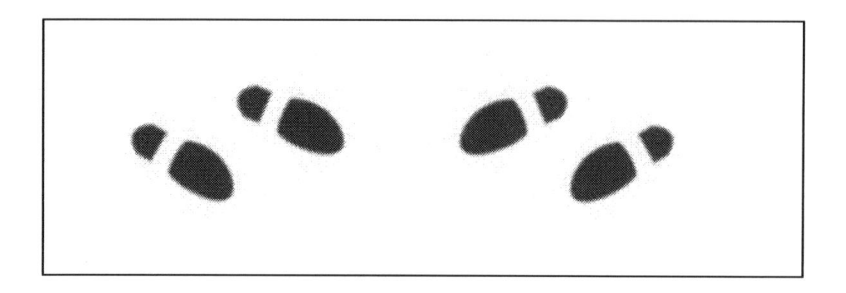

AUDIENCE

Notice that I did not say, "your right foot is ahead of your left foot" or "your left foot is ahead of your right." If I were facing left on stage then my left foot would be ahead, but if I were facing right then my right foot would be ahead. Standing this way keeps you open to the audience, helping to avoid the tendency to turn your back to the audience.

Actors rarely directly face an audience (except when the character is a narrator speaking directly to the audience). Usually they are talking and relating to other people on stage. The idea is for the audience to feel like they are peeking into a room or a scene through an invisible wall—often referred to as the "fourth wall."

Turning

A simple thing like turning on stage often becomes confusing. However, if you keep a few simple rules in mind you should be able to master it with a bit of practice:

> ➢ Your first step onto the stage is always made with your upstage foot.
> ➢ Always remember to stop with your upstage foot forward.
> ➢ Always turn toward the audience, not away from them.

- ➢ Avoid taking several little steps to make the turn. One move, pivoting on the balls of your feet is all that it takes.
- ➢ After you have turned, again make your first step with your upstage foot.

Do This: Have the actors pair up and do a drill on stance and turning. If room permits try having them partner with a person on the other side of the room and the whole group can do this at the same time. If space does not permit then just do a few pairs at a time.

Say This: I want you and your partner to first establish where the audience is, and then walk toward each other, remembering to step off on your upstage foot. Once you meet (center stage), stop with upstage foot forward and shake hands. Then, remembering to turn toward the audience, pivot on the balls of your feet so you are facing the opposite direction and then step off on the upstage foot again as you go back to your side of the room.

Sitting

We all have "signatures" when it comes to our personal idiosyncrasies. You can often identify someone by the sound of their footsteps, the way they sigh or a certain posture—even from a great distance. The same is true of the way we sit; both the act of sitting and the posture we assume once seated. First, let's see what we all look like.

Say This: Everyone stand up (wait for them to stand). Now, sit back down (wait for them to sit.) Now do it again. Stand up (wait). Sit down.

Now share observations about how people sit. Some fall into the chair, some reach back and feel for the chair, some look over their shoulders before sitting and some people bend over from the waist before lowering themselves into the chair. (You can demonstrate these if you like.)

Say This: Everyone stand up again. Stand nice and straight with good posture. Now, keeping your back as straight as possible, lower yourself onto the edge of the front of the chair and then slide back into the chair.

Do This: Have people again establish where the audience is and practice approaching their chair from several steps away. They should see the chair from a distance; then when they arrive at the chair, let the backs of their legs "find" the chair by brushing against it. Then without looking at it, they lower themselves into the chair. Try this several times.

> *Side Coach:* Remember to step off on your upstage foot. Turn toward the audience. Trust the chair without looking at it.

Now that we have gotten into the chair, take a moment to talk about how to position yourself once seated:

Men: While many men like to sit with their legs spread wide apart, this looks terrible from the audience. Men should have their legs closer together with about the width of their hand as space between their knees. Men may also cross their legs, but cross them so the middle of the calf rests on the knee rather than crossing them so the ankle rest on the knee. Make sure the bottom of the foot is not facing the audience. This will look much better.

Women: Obviously, keep legs together and preferably cross legs at the ankle. This is both a pleasing and modest position on stage.

Remember we are talking *neutral* here. The character we are playing my dictate a different way to stand, walk and sit.

Gestures

People generally fall into one extreme or the other when it comes to gesturing on stage: either they gesture too much or not at all. I don't usually advocate "planning" or rehearsing gestures. Most actors will discover the appropriate gestures as they discover the character. But still there are a few rules to keep in mind.

- ➢ Make most of your gestures with your upstage hands. This helps keep you open to the audience and prevents you from blocking your face with your gestures.
- ➢ Avoid "double pumping." That is, both hands doing the same thing at the same time.
- ➢ Gestures need to have motivation—just like all movement on stage. There needs to be a reason for the gesture.
- ➢ When not gesturing, simply relax your arms and your hands at the sides of your body. Avoid the habit of always crossing your arms or putting your hands in your pockets. These habits tend to make you look uncomfortable

on stage and subtly say to the audience: "I don't know what to do with my hands so I think I'll put them in my pockets."

Tip: If possible, always give actors a hand prop. It is amazing how many problems are solved by giving actors something to put in their hands. The prop can be something that helps identify who the character is or what they do. It will become an extension of their character. You will see your actors become much more comfortable on stage once they have a hand prop.

DEBRIEF

Try these questions for discussion:

Q: Did you learn anything about yourself as we went through this section?

Q: What will be the hardest part for you in turning these basics into habits?

Q: Will knowing these basics change the way you watch plays in the future?

Chapter 6

Acting Basics—Eye Focus

Our eyes, while a very small part of our body, are extremely important in the communication process, both in real life and on stage. The next section will help us understand just how important they are. I like to set up the next exercise without telling the group what it is about. They will figure it out before the exercise is done.

3-Way Conversation

Purpose: To show how our eyes communicate. To help each of us evaluate comfort levels in personal communication.

Say This: Everybody get a partner (encourage them to get someone they have not worked with yet). Spread out over the room—try to find some space so you are not too close to another team. Now sit either in a chair or on the floor back to back with your partner. There are three phases to this exercise.

Phase one is to simply begin having a conversation with your partner. Talk about whatever you want. Just remember to remain back to back.

Do This: Let them converse for at least two minutes. You want to give them enough time to get the conversation going. Make observations about comfort zones and notice who is enjoying this phase and who is not.

Say This: Okay stop! Now phase two. I want you to turn and face each other and continue your conversation; however, you are not allowed to make eye contact with your partner. Look wherever you like, except into their eyes. Go.

Do This: Once again, allow them to talk for a couple of minutes. Give them enough time to get used to the new setup. Continue to make observations as before.

Say This: Stop. Now, for phase three, this time I want you to continue your conversation but this time never take your eyes off of your partner's eyes. You are eyeball to eyeball the whole time.

Do This: Again, let them talk for a few minutes as you observe the different responses to the exercise.

After they have talked for a bit, stop them and have them turn their attention on you for a discussion. This exercise is very effective in helping people see just how important the eyes are in our communication.

> *Variation*: One thing you will inevitably hear is that none of the three phases is like "real life." In order to give the group a chance at "real life," I sometimes have them do a fourth phase of, "just have a normal conversation." What is fun about doing that is the group will be so focused on trying to figure out what normal is, that the fourth phase really is not normal after all!

DEBRIEF

You want people to begin to see that our eyes say things that go beyond words. So many truisms will come out in this discussion. You want the group to identify the fact that such things as honesty, love, hate, concern, confusion, intimacy and more are all communicated through the eyes.

Q: Which of the three phases was most comfortable? Uncomfortable? Why? (Note: There is not a right or wrong answer here. You will find that usually there are people who prefer one of the phases over another and often for very different reasons.)

Q: What does eye contact suggest?

Q: When you see really intense eye contact in a play or a movie what is about to happen? (Note: could be a kiss; could be a fight!)

Q: What does this exercise have to do with acting?

Eye Isolation

This exercise is optional, but a good one to further illustrate the power the eyes have in communicating ideas and emotions.

Purpose: To increase awareness of the eyes and their role in communication.

Do This: In advance prepare a list of common emotions. You will want at least four. Here are some examples: fear, love, hate and boredom.

Say This: Find a partner (or stay with the same partner from the previous exercise). For simply a point of reference assign one person as "A" and one as "B." (Give them a moment to do this). Person "A" is going to be the "sender" and person "B" is the receiver. Now, I am going to give the "A's" an emotion. They are then going to cover their face below the eyes with a piece of paper and then using only their eyes, and without speaking, try to convey that emotion to the "B's." The "B's" are to see if they can guess the emotion. So all the "A's" come up here and I will give you your emotion.

Do This: All the "A's" come to you and you assign them the first word (fear). Send them back to their partner and give them a couple minutes to try to communicate the word. Then repeat the exercise, switching roles and giving a word to the "B's." Let each person do two words.

> ***Side Coach***: *Remember to use only your eyes. Concentrate; don't allow yourself to get distracted or get the giggles.*

> ***Variation***: *As person "A" is sending the emotion, have person "B" communicate back with their eyes the same emotion. Now try it with person "B" sending back a contrasting emotion.*

DEBRIEF

> Ask these questions:
>
> Q: How many of you were successful in communicating the emotion to your partner?
>
> Q: If you guessed the wrong emotion, how far off were you?
>
> Q: Did you notice other parts of your body getting involved in the communication, almost involuntarily? What can you learn from this?

A few more notes on eye contact and focus on stage that should be discussed.

- ➢ Actors are often uncertain where to focus their eyes when they are on stage and not speaking. It is easy to figure out in a two-person conversation that you make eye contact with the person you are talking to. But if you are on stage and not part of the conversation…what then? As a general rule, eyes should follow the dialog. This is how you communicate to the audience that you are listening—by focusing on the person doing the talking. If you are not supposed to be involved in the conversation, then your character should have another reason for being on the stage, and the eyes are occupied in communicating that purpose (i.e. reading a magazine, eating, conversing silently with another character not in the audible dialog).

- ➢ Avoid "floor stabbing" and "ceiling stabbing." This is where you focus your eyes either up or down instead of at the person you are talking to. Sometimes an actor will do this momentarily, as if thinking to themselves, and as long as it is only a brief look away that is acceptable. But some actors turn this into a habit. It is almost as if they are looking for their lines on the floor or ceiling and this is to be avoided. This is especially noticeable in longer lines and monologues.

- ➢ When the character is thinking, turn the focus inwardly. It's almost as if the character is going within himself or herself to grasp for an idea. (In real life, when an actor forgets a line, this can be a clue to the audience.)

Think about the character's mind going into another room, searching for an idea.

- As we have already discussed, your eyes and your facial expressions are powerful communicators. The audience needs to see your thoughts mirrored on your face. While we don't want you to look at the audience (remember the fourth wall) we do want them to see your face in order to know what you are thinking. So make sure your face is up and open to the audience.

Chapter 7

Acting Basics — Voice Projection

You will notice that up to this point very little of our time and emphasis has had anything to do with speaking. This is intentional, to help drive home the point that acting is a visual medium and what we say with our bodies is as important as what we say with our mouths. But, now we shift to some vocal emphasis. We can have great body control but if we can't be heard then it is all for naught (unless we are preparing to become a mime)! Stage acting has changed over the years. It used to be that actors never relied on microphones to be heard. Actors were trained to project and prided themselves in their ability to be heard without amplification. Today almost every actor uses a microphone. While this technology has many benefits, it is still important for actors to know how to project their voices. Murphy's law does apply: "things will go wrong." And even the best sound equipment can't compensate for an actor that speaks too softly.

Breathing

Purpose: To show the importance of proper breathing and it's relationship to a strong voice on stage.

Say This: Everybody stand. Now take a big deep breath and then exhale. Okay, now do it again.

Do This: While they are taking their breaths watch for signs of incorrect breathing; it should be easy to spot. Correct breathing comes from the diaphragm, not the lungs. When a person takes a deep breath from the lungs, their shoulders go up and their chest pumps out. This does not give you a real deep breath. Conversely, if a person breathes from the diaphragm their stomach expands and they are able to hold much more air. After you have spotted some examples of good and bad breathing explain the difference to the group.

Say This: I want you to place your hand just below your rib cage and at the top of your stomach. Now breathe in and breathe out and see if you can feel your stomach going in and out on each breath. Think in terms of filling your body with air, filling from the bottom up. It might help you to inhale as if you were sipping through a straw. Now try inhaling slowly while I count to 5, then holding your breath for a 5 count and then exhale slowly over a 5 count. Ready, inhale, 1…2…3…4…5, hold, 1…2…3…4…5, exhale, 1…2…3…4…5… You can practice this at home and gradually increase the numbers. This will help you increase your breathing capacity and combat shortness of breath on stage. Here are some other things we can try together:

- Pant like a dog (do it); feel the stomach kick as you pant.
- Say with me: "HA, HA, HA." (do several times) Strive for a nice. loud accented *punch* on each "HA."

Notice that when we do this, we are not screaming. Screaming affects the throat and is most definitely the wrong way to project. Screaming will result in a sore throat and damaged voice. Proper projection may make your body tired but will put very little strain on the voice.

Tip: Sometimes you will encounter an actor who is unaware of the volume of their own voice and no matter how many times you tell them to project, they still speak at the same volume. You might try taking your group outside and pair them up in the parking lot. Have them recite words to a nursery rhyme back and forth to each other but with each line they speak they take one more step backwards away from each other. Sometimes this helps them to be aware of the need to pump up the volume.

Chapter 8

Acting Basics — Diction

You can have great projection but if we can't understand you because you have bad diction or you are talking too fast, then we have a problem. These next couple of exercises will help make us more aware of the need for good diction.

Pencil In The Mouth

Purpose: To force clear articulation of words and to force slower speech.

Do This: Make sure each person has a pen or pencil.

Say This: Take your pencil and place it lengthwise (like you're eating an ear of corn) between your front teeth and gently bite down to hold it in place. Now turn to the person next to you and begin having a conversation. Make sure you can be clearly understood as you talk around the obstacle in your mouth. (Let them try this for a couple minutes). Now take the pencil out of your mouth and continue the conversation as if the pencil was still in your mouth—not with clenched teeth but making your tongue and lips work just as hard as they were when you had the pencil in your mouth.

> **DEBRIEF**
>
> Ask the group the following questions:
>
> Q: What effect did the pencil have on your speech?
>
> Q: Could you tell a difference in the way you talked once you removed the pencil?

Tongue Twisters

Purpose: To force good articulation and rate of speech.

Do This: Prepare in advance several well-known tongue twisters. (You could write these on a chalkboard or have them on a handout.) Here a few you can use:

- Rubber baby buggy bumpers.

- She sells seashells by the seashore.
  The shells she sells are surely seashells.
  So if she sells shells on the seashore,
  I'm sure she sells seashore shells.

- How much wood would a woodchuck chuck
  if a woodchuck could chuck wood?
  He would chuck, he would, as much as he could,
  and chuck as much wood as a woodchuck would
  if a woodchuck could chuck wood.

- A skunk sat on a stump and thunk the stump stunk,
  but the stump thunk the skunk stunk.

- Peter Piper picked a peck of pickled peppers.
  Did Peter Piper pick a peck of pickled peppers?
  If Peter Piper picked a peck of pickled peppers,
  where's the peck of pickled peppers Peter Piper picked?

- Six thick thistle sticks. Six thick thistles stick.

Have the group say these out loud in unison. Try varying the rate getting faster without messing up. These are good for a few laughs but also serve to make the point.

DEBRIEF

Have a discussion about the importance of good diction. Identify common words that are often mispronounced or slurred in real life but from on stage would be hard to understand. One I often use is, "Let's go eat." In real life conversation it is often said fast and run together in one word like this: "lesgoeet." On stage in a large auditorium that might sound like, "squeet."

Hopefully this example and others like it will help your actors see the need for good, clear enunciation!

Chapter 9

Acting Basics — Memorization

I have to admit that memorizing lines is probably my least favorite thing to do as an actor. I dare say that most actors I know would agree! (However, I do know a few strange people that actually like to memorize!) Memorization can be hard work—no question. But with a few easy to learn techniques and with the right frame of mind, it can be some of your most productive time in preparing for a role. It is important to understand the difference between merely memorizing your lines and "owning your lines." An actor's goal is to know the lines so well that you don't have to stop and think, "what comes next?" The focus should be on character, not lines, when it comes time for performance. This idea of owning lines is brought home in the following discussion.

Say This: What are some things you know by heart? Things you can recite without stopping to ask, "what is the next word or sentence?"

Do This: Likely answers to the above question will be: The Lord's Prayer, The Pledge of Allegiance, Mary Had a Little Lamb, the alphabet, etc… Point out that these are things they own. Wouldn't it be nice if we knew our lines in a play as well as we know these things?

Steps in Memorizing

Here are some tried and true steps in memorizing a script.

- ➢ Read the script, read the script, read the script!!! At the risk of being redundant—read the script. Read it first to get a good understanding of the story. Read it again to gain insight into your character. Read it again for understanding of other characters and their interaction with your character. Read it until you can tell the story of the script in your own words.
- ➢ Highlight your lines so they stand out on the page.
- ➢ Using a blank sheet of paper, cover all the lines and slide the paper down —a line at time—as you work on each of your lines.
- ➢ Memorize out loud. Say your lines and the cue lines (the other person's lines) out loud.

- Only after you can respond with the correct line, word for word, do you move on to the next line.
- Memorize on your feet. Keeping your body moving gets your blood pumping, helping to keep you alert and focused.

The methods above are not the only methods that work. Many people have great success using a voice recorder. This is a great method, especially when finding someone to run lines with you is inconvenient. If using a voice recorder, be sure to record not only your lines but the cue lines as well, so you will still be accustomed to hearing and learning those cues!

You need to be aware that memorization comes in phases. There is the "on paper" phase, where you are working from reading the lines. You need to graduate from this to the "audible phase," where you run the lines with another person to get you accustomed to hearing the lines. Next there is the "with movement" phase, where you incorporate your blocking (stage blocking is the term used for the movement given to an actor) and stage action with the lines. The final phase is "what will you really do in front of a live audience?" This is where we find out if you will succumb to stage fright or be able to truly enjoy being in the moment and acting in front of people. I find it a good idea to have a small audience of family and friends at a dress rehearsal in order to test the performers in this area, as well as allowing them to experience a live audience before the real thing on opening night. Another option would be to perform the show before small group, class or at a retirement home.

Tip: Line memorization is a great place to practice the basic movements we talked about earlier. Pace, stepping off on the upstage foot and then turning toward the audience. This will help make those simple movements a habit! If the actor knows the stage blocking ahead of time then practicing the blocking in conjunction with the line memorization helps to learn it all at once!

One question that inevitably comes up on the subject of memorization is, "Do I have to memorize my lines word for word?" The answer to this is always YES! Why? Here are a few good reasons:

- You are not the playwright (well...unless you are the playwright). In most situations you are performing a published work and so copyright law will usually prohibit you from making changes without the author/publisher's consent.

- Learning lines also involves learning cue lines. If the actor I am on stage with changes their line then there is a good chance he throw me off track with the paraphrased line. You should never surprise other actors on stage by doing or saying things that were not rehearsed, and paraphrasing a line is a sure way to surprise your fellow actors.
- One reason actors will want to change a line is usually this excuse: "I would never say it that way." My response is, "So what? You are not the character. The character would say it that way so you need to let the character say it that way—not you!"
- On the rare occasion where a line change is permitted (localizing a play, adapting for gender, etc.) any line changes are agreed upon in advance so they become a permanent part of the script.

One of the biggest fears an actor has is forgetting his/her lines. So let's address that. What should you do if you forget your lines or if you are on stage with someone who has forgotten their lines?

- *Don't panic.* I know that is easier said than done! But if you follow the memorization methods outlined above, you will know the story and thus know what is supposed to happen next. Stop and take a breath and recall what you just said and what is supposed to happen next. Often this will get you right back on track. One reason that actors go blank is because they stop being "in the moment." They get distracted by thinking ahead or replaying a scene that did not go well and suddenly they are not really listening and connected to what is happening now.

- In the memorization methods described above you were to say not only your line out loud but the cue line as well. One of the benefits of this is that you will discover that you have actually memorized the cue line—even though you were not consciously trying to do so. This is of great benefit on stage. If you are on stage with someone who has gone blank you have several options:

    - Take their line for them, paraphrasing it slightly to make it your own.

    - Ask a question that helps them recall what they are supposed to say.

    - Drop hints of information in ad-libbed lines that help remind the actor of what they are supposed to say.

Remember: the goal when things go wrong is to get back on track—not invent a whole new script. A common tendency when an actor blanks is to just say any line they can think of, even if that means jumping ahead several pages. This only escalates the problem—now not only do you have to try to get back on track but you also have to figure out how to go back and pick up the information in the script that has been skipped. Better to take a few seconds of painful silence than to leave out important information that confuses or thwarts the storyline. Often the few seconds of silence will seem like an eternity to you but the audience may not even notice.

Finally, remember that old TV commercial for deodorant that used the slogan "never let them see you sweat?" The audience should never know that you made a mistake. Learn to cover your mistakes. Make your mistakes look like they were "supposed to happen that way." Say the wrong line with gusto and then worry about fixing it. Don't say, "oops!" If you walk on the stage at the wrong time, cover your mistake by making it look like you were supposed to enter then. The audience will usually never be aware of your mistakes—and thus you should never talk about them with anyone except the cast. You want the audience to believe what they are seeing is really happening—when you talk about the things that go wrong with audience members, you are ruining the very effect you were trying to create.

DEBRIEF

This is often a section that generates quite a bit of discussion. The fear of blanking on stage is very real. Take time here to allow people to voice their concerns and encourage each other in this area.

Chapter 10

Acting Basics — Characterization

Now the fun begins. Up to this point most of the basics we have talked about are just that—the basics. The real fun and creative part of being an actor is in creating believable characters on stage. This is where we get to use our imaginations; where we revert back to what many of us did so well in our childhood—pretend. As we get older we tend to lose the knack for playing and pretending. We view that as childishness. But the very freedom that children have to lose themselves in a make-believe world is the very essence of real and believable characters on stage. We need to recapture that!

"Being" not "Acting"

Purpose: To free our imaginations and move beyond stereotypes to create believable characters.

Do This: In setting up this exercise it is important that you not give any preparation time to the group for the first phase. Part of the learning experience in this exercise is the contrast between the lack of prep time for the first phase contrasted with prep time for the second phase.

Say This: Without thinking too much about it, I want everybody to pretend that you are 80 years old. Now get up and mill about the room and talk to each other as 80-year-old people.

Do This: Give the group about 3-5 minutes to play with this. During this time observe what they are doing. If your group is typical, you will see a lot of people doing pretty much the same thing: stooped over posture, trembling hands, slight limp and shaky voice. When you ask them to stop, don't allow them to discuss the experience yet.

Say This: Stop. Okay, now everybody take a seat. Please spread out in the room so you are not too close to another person. I don't want you to be distracted by anyone during the next phase of this exercise. We are going to become the 80-year-old person again, but this time we are going to approach it differently. I am going to give you a series of questions and statements designed to help think through what it would be like to be 80 years old, and I want you to work through the answers in your imagination—don't answer out loud. This portion of the exercise is non-verbal on your part; I will be the only one talking. If some of the questions cause you to want to answer out loud or contribute a witty comment—resist the temptation. Please take the process seriously.

Before we begin you need to make a decision: are you going to be "you" at 80 years old or are you going to become another person? Now before we begin, let me set the scene. I want you to imagine you are in your bedroom alone, sitting in front of a full-length mirror. Take a moment to see the room ... because I will be asking you several questions about your body and physical condition you might want to imagine you are sitting in your underwear—it's okay; there is no one else in the room. Also keep in mind that not everyone who is 80 years old is an invalid—some are very active, vital people. You decide what kind of person you want to create. Allow your body to change as we consider each part of it. Okay, close your eyes, take a deep breath and let's begin. (Note: After each question below allow a moment of silence for them to think through the answer. It helps to make your voice as relaxing and soothing as possible so that people can focus their attention. These questions are only suggestions—feel free to create your own.)

- Start with your feet. What do they look like? See the color and texture of your skin. Scrunch your toes. Make your feet 80 years old.
- Move up to your ankles. Feel free to move them around. Do they move easily?
- Now move up to your calves and shins. Make them 80 years old.
- Next are your knees. As you age body parts that are joints, bear in mind that these are often problem spots in older people. Arthritis may be an issue. Is it for you?
- Move to your thighs. Make them 80 years old.
- Now your hips. Many older people end up having hip replacement surgery. How about you?
- Take a trip up your back. One vertebra at a time. Make it 80 years old. If you decide that you are stooped over, consider that the tension in being stooped over is *up* not *down*. You are trying to stand up straight; it's just that your body doesn't go and won't go any straighter.
- Consider your stomach and chest. Are there scars? Have you been under the surgeon's knife? Consider your internal organs. Your heart? Your stomach and digestive track? Your lungs? How is your breathing? Can you hear it?

- Look at your hands. See color and texture. How is your grip when you make a fist?
- Now consider your forearms, elbows and upper arms. How does your skin hang on your upper arms?
- Now move to your shoulders. Square or rounded?
- See your neck. See how the skin hangs. See the wrinkles.
- How many chins can you count when you look in the mirror?
- Look at your face. Consider: Glasses? Hearing aids? False teeth? Wrinkles? Hair color? Baldness?

We could go on and on just on the physical aspects, but now let's move on to other areas for consideration.

- Are you married?
- If married, is your spouse living?
- Do you have children? How many?
- Where do you live? In your own home? Retirement home? With one of your children?
- Is immediate family nearby or far away? How often do you see family?
- What time do you get up in the morning?
- What do you eat for breakfast?
- What will you do today? Visit people? Volunteer? Stay home and watch TV?
- How would you describe yourself? Happy? A curmudgeon? Content? Bitter?
- What was the happiest day or time of your life?
- What was the saddest day or time of your life?
- How often do you see a doctor? Are you on a daily medication?
- At the age of 80 you must have thought a lot about the end of your life. What are your general thoughts about death? Fear it? Looking forward to it?
- What are your regrets?
- Finish this sentence: "If I could do one more thing before I die it would be _____."

There are many more questions I could ask you but you have enough now to move on to the next phase of this exercise. I want you to all imagine now that we are a room full of the 80 year olds you have just been creating in your imaginations. We are going to imagine that we are all gathered together for a birthday party for a friend named Harold. You are all getting ready for his arrival at the party. When he comes in we will sing Happy Birthday to him. Okay, let's get ready. Go!

Do This: Let them get up and move about the room. You might want to give them some ideas to motivate them. Allow enough time for them to really get into and interact with each other. After a few minutes tab somebody to be "Harold" and have him enter the room so everyone can sing Happy Birthday.

> 🗣 ***Side Coach***: *Greet your friends, some who you have not seen for a long time. Introduce people to each other. Discuss how you know Harold. Somebody needs to organize the group for Harold's arrival. Harold is here!*

DEBRIEF: Discuss with the group what was the difference between the first time they were 80 and the second time. What made the difference? How many were doing "themselves" at 80? What is the difference between a caricature and a real person? Share observation and contrast between the first and second phase.

> 👁 ***Variation***: *The above exercise can also be tweaked and adapted to different ages. Try having the group become all 5-year-olds. Another adaptation of the exercise is to have the group people attending a large event. (i.e. have them all be the attending the Super Bowl or a pop concert.)*

Character Analysis Worksheet

Included in the handouts at the end of the book is a "Character Analysis Worksheet." Photocopy and hand these out to the group for discussion. These sheets are intended to "jumpstart" the character analysis process. Developing believable characters on stage is a process that actors study and work on all the time and certainly takes more work and practice than can be accomplished in a short portion of a day-long workshop. However, if we can get the participants to ask two basic questions, we have done our job: "Who am I?" and "What do I want?" The next exercise will help to emphasize this point.

A/B Role-Play

Purpose: To introduce the idea of conflict in drama. To help actors discover "motivation" in preparing a scene.

Say This: Everyone get a partner. Appoint one of you as person "A" and the other as person "B." As you know, drama is based on conflict. A play in which everyone agrees with each other all the time would be pretty boring. However, conflict doesn't necessarily mean fighting or arguing. It simply means that you want something and there is something keeping you from getting what you want —also referred to as an "obstacle." So now we are going to give you a chance to work through some conflicts. First you need to know who you are—and the answer to that is you are YOU, you are playing yourself, except as modified by the conflict (if I say you don't like coffee and you really do then you have to pretend that you really don't like it!). Here is your first conflict:

> - Person "A" has just won an all expenses paid trip to Europe. The vacation of a lifetime! You will be flown into Paris and then tour all over Europe for two weeks. You also get to bring one other person along and you have chosen your partner, Person "B."
> - Person "B" is Person "A's" very good friend and would love nothing better than to go on this trip to Europe. However, there is one slight problem—you are terrified of flying. You have vowed to never get on an airplane for as long as you live. The very thought of getting on a plane makes you ill.

Now go ahead and role play.

Do This: While they act this out, you should observe and see how much they "get into" this exercise. You will notice that most will not be thinking about "acting" and thus are often very natural and uninhibited. They will be using body language, facial expressions, gestures, vocal inflections and in general doing a very believable job of acting. This is all good stuff and needs to be affirmed. So stop them and affirm them. Also point out how easy it was to do this once they knew what their purpose was and totally understood the conflict. Make sure they get the connection between that and working on a play.

Then go on and do another one. Here is a suggestion:

Say This: Let's do another one:

> - Person "B" is single and just about 6 weeks ago met Mr. (or Miss) Right. This person is the person of your dreams. You are head over heels in love with each other. Even though you have only been dating for a few weeks you have received (or given) a marriage proposal. You are on a fast track to get married. You can't wait to tell your friend, Person "A," all about it!
> - Person "A" thinks this is a huge mistake. This is all happening way too fast. You think Person "B" needs to slow down—way down! And perhaps you know something about Mr. or Miss Right that if they knew, might just change their mind. Try to convince them not to go through with this crazy marriage plan!

After they have played this out, once again discuss this and share observations.

Out of Context

Purpose: To help actors discover motivation and meanings beyond what is explicit in written dialog.

Do This: There are short dialog samples in the handout section in this book. Photocopy them, making enough for each participant working in pairs. It is perfectly okay that several pairs will have the same dialog—in fact that makes this exercise even more interesting. Have the actors partner up and then distribute the dialogs.

Say This: As you are learning today, there is more to acting than just simply memorizing and speaking lines. Acting involves our bodies, our eyes, our imaginations and more. The dialogs you have in your hands are out of context. Just reading them raises all kinds of who, what, where, when and why questions. I want you and your partner to answer those questions. This is called the subtext. Discover or make up who and where these people are. Why are they saying the things they say? Give the scene a context. Then I want you to memorize the lines (the scenes are very short) and then you will perform them for the group. Your performance in context should "fill in the blanks" for the audience. However, you are only allowed to say what is on the page. You may not add any lines or words. You can and should add action. Keep in mind that you may need long pauses between lines and possibly even in the middle of a line in order for your context to be communicated. You have about 10 minutes to work on this and then the performance will begin.

Do This: Let them go to work. You may want to walk around and eavesdrop on the teams as they work, to make sure they are understanding the assignment. After the 10 minutes are up call everyone together and have groups take turns performing the scenes. Affirm all the different interpretations that come out of the scenes. This exercise usually opens a lot of people's eyes in terms of understanding the difference between just saying words and acting from an understanding of context and motivation.

> *Variation: It can be great fun to assign actual character pairings to the dialogs and see what they do with them. Don't tell the audience who they are but see if they can guess based on what the actors do with the scenes. Examples: Jack and Jill, Little Red Riding Hood and the Big Bad Wolf, Lewis and Clark, Antony and Cleopatra, Adam and Eve, David and Goliath, Romeo and Juliet, etc...*

DEBRIEF: Discuss how they decided on the context. How did the context affect or change the way a line was said (especially if there were very different interpretations of the same scene)?

Story Improvisations

If time permits, give the actors one more opportunity to try to put it all together—body control, movement, eye contact, projection, diction and characterization. A great way to do this is with story improvisations.

Purpose: To allow the actors to be creative and make up scenes. To practice the acting skills they have learned in the workshop.

Do This: Prepare in advance a list of locations that can be used as the basis for a simple story. You will need one location for each group of four or five people. Here is a list you can use (or make up your own):

- parking lot
- grocery store
- hotel lobby
- police station
- amusement park
- classroom

Break the participants up into groups of 4 or 5 people (or use the same animal groups formed at the beginning of the workshop).

Say This: Now you are going to do a little group improvisation. I want you to make up and act out a simple story. I do mean simple; don't make this complicated. A story has a beginning, a middle and an end. Establish a where, a who, and a what. I will give you the "where" and you do the rest. These stories should only last about 3 minutes. Keep it simple. Each person in your group should have a distinct character and at least one line of dialog. You don't need to write it out. It is improvisation; just make it up as you go like you did in the A/B Role Play exercise. You will have about 5-10 minutes to prepare and then we will come together for performance.

Do This: Go around to each group and assign the location. While they are figuring out their stories you should listen and observe to make sure every group is understanding the exercise. You might need to give some simple story examples. (i.e: A man is shopping, he sees another person shoplifting. He confronts the man who denies he did anything wrong. The clerk is called, who then calls the cops and they take the man away in handcuffs). After the preparation, call the group together for performance. Give plenty of affirmation and perhaps some mild critique after each performance. The critique should point out reminders about things like projection, basic staging (could we see everyone?), and motivation.

Chapter 11

Putting it All Together

If you made it this far, take a deep breath, pat yourself on the back and say a prayer of thanksgiving. You did it! The hard part of the workshop is over.

You might want to go back and revisit Chapter 2 and the section titled, **What Does it Take to Make it Work?** Before you send everyone home it is a good idea to outline what happens next!

Here would be a great time to craft a mission statement. Identify the purpose of your drama troupe. Are you primarily focused on drama for your school, church or your organization? Will you be mainly using drama for special occasions (Christmas and Easter)? Or is touring your main goal? Knowing this is essential to planning your goals.

How are you going to be organized? Will the person who directs the plays also be the organizer of all the drama events or will that responsibility be shared? How often will you meet? Will your meetings be training, rehearsal or both? Will you do social things as a group? (Going to see plays as a group is a great learning and bonding experience!)

One thing to keep in mind is that drama troupes only seem to flourish when they have the payoff of performance. So set up a schedule of performances as soon as you can. The team will be excited to know that there is a performance looming. They won't want to come to regular meetings if there are no performances upcoming.

Hopefully this has been a great launching pad for your group. May your efforts be rewarded…*dramatically!*

Handouts

Stage Diagram

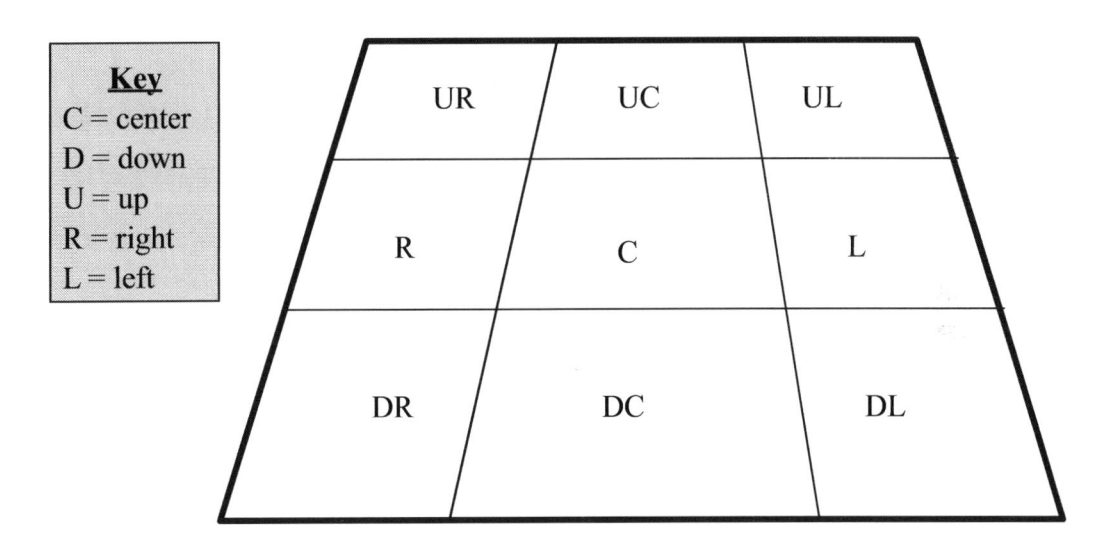

Key
C = center
D = down
U = up
R = right
L = left

UR	UC	UL
R	C	L
DR	DC	DL

Audience

Stance

Audience

Character Analysis Worksheet

Analyze the script to determine these clues to your character:

- ➢ What the character does.
- ➢ What the character says.
- ➢ What the other characters say about him/her and their purpose in saying it.
- ➢ What actions are suggested in the character's lines.
- ➢ What comments and descriptions are offered in the playwright's stage directions.

Based on the information in the script and *clues derived from the director's interpretation of the play*, it is now the actor's task to make the character a real person.

History

Consider the background and history of the character (feel free to add to the list):

• name	• age	• birthplace	• appearance
• parents	• siblings	• religion	• education
• world history	• ethnic background	• occupation	• athletics
• physical problems	• hobbies	• skills	• spouse
• children	• social standing	• deaths	• honors

Emotional Make-up

Consider the emotional makeup of the character. Evaluate the character in the following areas (feel free to add to the list). Consider the hows and whys of each area that apply.

• aggressive	• passive	• angry	• impulsive
• happy-go-lucky	• logical	• depressed	• vindictive
• reflective	• tactful	• direct	• fearful
• hopeful	• apathetic	• lonely	• anxious
• impatient	• wishy washy	• evasive	• loving

Questions to Consider

What does my character want?

What is my character willing to do to get it?

How does my character feel about the other characters in the play?

Is my character a protagonist or an antagonist?

Does my character like himself/herself? Why or why not?

Does my character change during the play? How and why?

What motivates or drives my character?

How does my character spend a typical day?

Is my character on attack or defense?

What are my character's greatest strengths? Weaknesses?

Why and how is my character important to this play?

Which of the other characters in the play is your character's favorite? Least favorite? Why?

What are my character's goals and aspirations?

Who or what gets in the way of my character reaching his/her goal (the antagonist)?

How is my character different from myself? In what ways is he/she the same?

SAMPLE DIALOG #1[1]

A. What are you doing here?

B. I brought this.

A. Yes, I see.

B. Good.

A. Now what?

B. Maybe it's time to go.

A. Oh.

---

[1] Dialog #1 written by Tom Long, Friends of the Groom. Used by permission.

SAMPLE DIALOG #2

A: So now what do we do?

B: I'm really hungry.

A: Well, what about me?

B: It won't be much longer.

A: Great!

B: Come on baby!

A: I'll start a fire.

SAMPLE DIALOG #3

A: I thought I'd find you here.

B: I can't stand it!

A: What are you going to do?

B: I know what I'd like to do!

A: That won't solve anything.

B: I'd feel better.

A: No, you wouldn't. Is this the right time?

B: Not yet.

SAMPLE DIALOG # 4

A: You always said I could ask you anything.

B: Yeah, but not that . . . that's different.

A: How? You did it, didn't you?

B: Why do you jump to that conclusion?

A: Because of that.

B: Oh, I forgot about that. Maybe I should I hide it.

A: Here. It's okay. It's safe with me.

Acknowledgements

Most of the content found on these pages is not original. These exercises and teachings are hand-me-downs from years of experience, classes, books, and teachers. I've learned so much from former drama teachers and theater directors going all the way back to childhood productions in church, high school, college and professional productions. So, I am forever grateful to Hilda Hamilton, Linda Deretich, John Lee Welton, and Charles M. Tanner. I have learned so much from each of you and hope the words on these pages reflect the quality of the time and energies that you poured into me—and so many others. Thank you!

About The Author

Chuck Neighbors is an actor and writer. For over 45 years he has toured throughout North America as well as to 18 countries on 6 continents around the world. His most popular show, a one-man dramatic adaptation of Charles Sheldon's classic **In His Steps,** has been featured on radio and television and performed before thousands of audiences. Chuck has performed in theaters, churches, gymnasiums, airplane hangars and even on board a submarine. As a writer, Chuck's published works include 11 books of theater scripts including **The Comfort Zone** and **In The Moment** (Lillenas) and **Power Plays** (six volumes, Baker Books). He recently wrote and published **Get Me to the Church in Rhyme,** a collection of limericks on God, faith and the church. Chuck is married to Lorie and they make their home in Salem, Oregon.

Made in the USA
Las Vegas, NV
08 March 2023